SPACE!

THE DWARF PLANET
PLUTO

KRISTI LEW

Marshall Cavendish
Benchmark
New York

Marshall Cavendish Benchmark
99 White Plains Road
Tarrytown, New York 10591
www.marshallcavendish.us

Library of Congress Cataloging-in-Publication Data
Lew, Kristi.
  The dwarf planet Pluto / by Kristi Lew.
    p. cm. -- (Space!)
  Summary: "Describes the dwarf planet Pluto, including its history, its composition, and
its role in the solar system"--Provided by publisher.
  Includes bibliographical references and index.
  ISBN 978-0-7614-4243-1
  1. Pluto (Dwarf planet)--Juvenile literature. I. Title.
  QB701.L49 2010
  523.49'22--dc22
  2008037272

Editor: Karen Ang
Publisher: Michelle Bisson
Art Director: Anahid Hamparian
Series Design by Daniel Roode
Production by nSight, Inc.

Front cover: A computer illustration of Pluto
Title page: A Hubble Space Telescope image shows Pluto, Charon, and two other moons.
Photo research by Candlepants Incorporated
Front cover: Photo Researchers Inc.
Cover Photo: Friedrich Saurer / Alamy Images

The photographs in this book are used by permission and through the courtesy of:
AP Images: NASA, 1, 54; Matt York, 19; 35; John Raoux, 52. *Getty Images:* National
Geographic, 4, 5; D'Arco Editori, 25; Antonio M. Rosario, 58. *Super Stock:* Pixtal, 7; Digital
Vision Ltd., 12, 44. *Photo Researchers Inc.:* Friedrich Saurer, 15, 38; Science Source, 22,
23, 47, 50, 56; Shigemi Numazawa / Atlas Photo Bank, 27; Mark Garlick, 30, 46; Detlev van
Ravenswaay, 34, 40, 41; The International Astronomical Union / Martin Kornmesser, 57.
The Image Works: Mary Evans Picture Library, 16. *Corbis:* Bettmann, 18; Denis Scott, 36,
37; NASA/Roger Ressmeyer, 55. *The Bridgeman Art Library:* Musee Conde, Chantilly,
France / Lauros / Giraudon, 20. *Art Resource, NY:* Erich Lessing, 32. *NASA:* Lunar and
Planetary Institute, 21, 43. *SOHO:* NASA and ESA, 48, 49. Solar System chart on page 9 by
Mapping Specialists © Marshall Cavendish Corporation.
Printed in Malaysia
123456

CONTENTS

1

WHAT IS PLUTO?

For more than 75 years, our Solar System had nine planets: Mercury, Venus, Earth, Mars, Jupiter, Saturn, Uranus, Neptune, and Pluto. However, in August 2006, the International Astronomical Union (IAU) defined what a planet is. Pluto did not meet the requirements of a regular planet and was reclassified as a dwarf planet. The IAU is a group of more than nine thousand scientists from all over the world who study stars, planets, and other objects in space. Scientists who study space and the objects in it are called **astronomers**.

So now our Solar System has only eight planets. These eight planets and the other space objects that make up our Solar System are in a **galaxy** called the Milky Way. Our galaxy, and many others, are scattered throughout the universe. The universe is a very big place. It contains all of the **matter** and energy that exists. Matter is anything that you can physically touch. An apple, a desk, and the air are all examples of matter—and so are you.

The Milky Way is a galaxy that is home to our Solar System, a collection of comets, meteors, and asteroids, hundreds of billions of stars, and much more that we have yet to discover.

THE UNIVERSE AND ITS GALAXIES

Astronomers are not exactly sure how big the universe really is, however, they are almost certain that it is getting bigger. The Milky Way's next door neighbor is a galaxy called Andromeda. Even though Andromeda is the closest galaxy to ours, it is still more than 2 million **light-years** away. A light-year is the number of miles that light can travel in one year. That is a lot of miles because light can travel at 186,000 miles (299,338 kilometers) per second. That means that one light-year is almost 6 trillion miles (9.6 trillion km). So Andromeda may be the closest galaxy to us, but it is still very, very far away. And the distance between our galaxy and Andromeda continues to get bigger and bigger.

Galaxies are groups of stars, dust, and gas held together by **gravity**. Gravity is a force that attracts one object to another. It is what keeps you and everyone else on the surface of Earth instead of flying off into space. About 4.5 billion years ago, when astronomers believe our Solar System was formed, gravity pulled chunks of space rock, dust, and gas together to make the Sun, Earth, and the other planets. Gravity also causes Earth to **orbit,** or travel, around the Sun. The Moon also moves around Earth because of gravity.

nauts in space experience
little gravity when they
r from a planet or moon.
they are outside of their
craft, they are often
red, or linked, to keep them
floating away.

Anything that has **mass** has a gravitational force—even you. Earth's gravity pull keeps you on the surface of the planet, but you exert a force on Earth, too. However, the amount of gravitational force exerted, or used, by an object is related to the object's mass. The more massive an object, the more gravity it exerts. Because Earth is much more massive than you, it pulls on you harder than you pull on it. The Sun is the most massive object in our Solar System and it exerts a tremendous gravitational force on the planets and other objects surrounding it. Just as Earth's gravity keeps you from flying off into space, the Sun's gravity keeps the planets in orbit. The Sun's gravitational force holds our Solar System together.

Gravitational force is also affected by the distance between two objects. Distance between objects weakens gravitational force. Even though the Sun exerts a much higher gravitational force than Earth does, the distance between Earth and the Sun keeps the Sun's gravity from grabbing us off of the face of the planet.

MASS VERSUS WEIGHT

Mass is the amount of matter in an object. To better understand mass, imagine a bowling ball and golf ball. The bowling ball contains more matter than the golf ball, making it more massive. Because of this higher amount of mass, if you weigh these objects, the bowling ball will weigh much more than the golf ball.

But mass and weight are not the same. An object's weight depends on how hard gravity is pulling on that object. That means that an object's weight can be different in different locations. For example, the Moon is much smaller than Earth. Therefore, it exerts less gravitational force. Because there is less gravity on the Moon, a bowling ball will weigh less on the Moon than it does on Earth even though the ball contains the same amount of matter. To prevent confusion, scientists prefer to use the term mass instead of weight to describe an object because location will not change an object's mass.

THE SOLAR SYSTEM

Our Sun is the closest star to Earth. It is classified as a yellow dwarf star. But compared to other stars, it is really medium-sized. It looks much bigger than the other stars in the sky because it is so close to Earth. In outer space, however, even things that are considered close are very far away. In fact, the Sun is more

Of the nine original planets, Pluto was the smallest and the farthest from the Sun.

than 93 million miles from Earth. Because outer space is so big, astronomers measure distance using a unit called the astronomical unit (A.U.) so that they do not have to use such large numbers. One A.U. is the mean distance from Earth to the Sun, about 93 million miles (149 million km).

Astronomers divide the planets of our Solar System into three different groups—the inner, rocky planets; the gas giants; and the ice dwarfs of the **Kuiper** (pronounced *Ki-per*) **Belt**. Earth, Venus, Mercury, and Mars are the inner, rocky planets. These four planets are sometimes called terrestrial planets, too. Jupiter, Saturn, Uranus, and Neptune are the gas giants. These planets are also called Jovian planets. The gas giants are made up almost entirely of gas. The Kuiper Belt is a section of space that is beyond the eight planets of our Solar System. Pluto is the largest object in the Kuiper Belt.

Moons

The Sun and the planets are not the only objects in our Solar System, however. Many planets, including our own, also have moons. A moon can also be called a satellite. Satellites are objects that orbit a larger body. Earth's moon is a natural satellite. Satellites can also be artificial, or human-made. The Hubble Space Telescope is an example of an artificial satellite. The Hubble orbits Earth. It flies 346 miles (557 km) above the surface and goes around the planet every 97 minutes.

Earth has only one moon, but other planets have many more. In fact, there are a total of 144 moons in our Solar System. At the moment, Jupiter holds the record for the highest number of moons. It has 63 natural satellites. Scientists are sure that 49 of the objects orbiting Jupiter are, indeed, moons. They suspect another 14 are also, but they are still studying these. Astronomers continue to search for more moons around many of the planets.

Asteroids, Comets, and Meteoroids

Our Solar System also contains thousands of what scientists call "small solar system bodies." These objects include thousands of **asteroids**, **comets**, and **meteoroids**. Asteroids are rocky bodies that can be anywhere from a few hundred feet to a few hundred miles wide. Most of the asteroids in our Solar System orbit the Sun between Mars and Jupiter. This area is called the asteroid belt.

Comets tend to stay farther away from the Sun than the asteroids. Comets are made up of leftover ice, frozen gases, and dust that was not captured and made into one of the planets when the Solar System was formed. Because of their ice and dirt content, comets are sometimes called "dirty snowballs." The ice and frozen gases that make up a comet warm up when the

Comets are some of the celestial bodies, or space objects, that can be seen with the unaided eye from Earth. Detailed images such this are taken by strong telescopes and satellites.

comet gets close to the Sun. When this happens, some of the ice and frozen gases can change from a solid into a gas. This process is called sublimation.

Solar winds—gases that rush outward from the Sun—push these gases into a stream that follows along behind the head of the comet. This stream is called the comet's tail. It is also how comets got their name. The word comet comes from the Latin word *cometa*, which means "long-hair." Some comet tails can stretch as far as 93 million miles (149 million km) long.

Scientists believe that there are around 100 million comets in the Solar System. Comets follow a regular orbit around the Sun, just like planets and other bodies. But the length of each comet's orbit can vary enormously. Astronomers have divided comets into two types—short-period comets and long-period comets. Short-period comets make one complete trip around the Sun in 200 years or less. Halley's Comet is an example of a short-period comet. It comes close enough to Earth for us to view it every 75 to 76 years. The last time it was seen from Earth was 1986. Scientists predict that it will reappear around 2061.

Some short-period comets have an orbital period of less than 20 years, which is relatively fast. These comets are pulled into the inner Solar System by Jupiter's gravity, so they are called Jupiter Family comets. But not all comets move around the Sun this fast. It can take other comets as long as 30 million years to complete their trip. These comets are called long-period comets.

Like asteroids, meteoroids are also rocky bodies orbiting the Sun. Meteoroids are much smaller than asteroids, however. When a meteoroid enters Earth's **atmosphere** (the layer of gases that surrounds a planet), it is called a meteor. As a meteor passes though the atmosphere, it heats up and burns. This leaves a visible streak across the sky. People often call these streaks "falling" or "shooting" stars. But they really are not stars at all, just space "dirt" hitting our atmosphere. Sometimes Earth passes though the path of a comet that has left a lot of dust behind. When this happens, a lot of meteoroids hit Earth's atmosphere all at one time and we see a meteor shower.

Most meteors completely burn up in Earth's atmosphere. But occasionally a piece will survive its fiery flight and reach the ground. When a meteor makes it to Earth's surface, it is called a meteorite. More than 100 meteorites fall to Earth every year. Because they come from space and are made of the same material that other space bodies are made of, meteorites can provide astronomers with a lot of information about the rest of our Solar System.

WHAT IS PLUTO?

So where does this leave Pluto? It is no longer a planet, but it is not a star, an asteroid, a comet, or a meteoroid. Actually, Pluto now belongs to another group of Solar System objects. Astronomers have decided that Pluto is a dwarf planet. They have already identified the first five dwarf planets—Pluto, Ceres, Haumea, Makemake, and Eris. There are also at least forty other objects that scientists think belong to this group, too. They suspect there are even more than two hundred other dwarf planets out there just waiting to be found.

Ceres orbits the Sun in the asteroid belt between Mars and Jupiter. Until 2006, when the IAU added the new dwarf planet classification, Ceres was considered the largest asteroid in the asteroid belt. Now, like Pluto, it is classified as a dwarf planet. Ceres is about 2.77 A.U., or 258 million miles (415 million km), from the Sun.

Pluto and Eris, on the other hand, are quite a bit farther from the Sun than Ceres. On average, Pluto is 39.5 A.U. away from the

A computer illustration shows what scientists think Ceres looks like.

Sun. That is 3.67 billion miles (5.9 billion km)! In other words, Pluto is almost forty times farther from the Sun than the Earth is.

Pluto has a very strange orbit, however. Most of the time, Pluto is farther from Earth than Neptune is. But sometimes Pluto sneaks inside Neptune's orbit so that Neptune is farther away than Pluto. The last time Neptune and Pluto switched places and Pluto came closer to Earth than Neptune was in 1979. Twenty years later, Pluto went back to being the outermost planet (it was still classified as a planet in 1999). In 1989, when Pluto got as close to Earth—and to the Sun—as it ever gets, it was almost a billion miles closer to Earth than it was when it was discovered in 1930.

FINDING PLUTO

In 1905, Percival Lowell, the founder of the Lowell Observatory in Flagstaff, Arizona, started looking for a ninth planet in our Solar System. Because of the strange paths of Uranus's and Neptune's orbits around the Sun, Lowell was convinced that something lay beyond the eighth planet.

This was not the first time an astronomer searched for a new planet based on the way it made another planet move around the Sun. Uranus's orbit also gave away Neptune's existence. The way Uranus traveled told astronomers that another planet's gravity was influencing its path. By studying Uranus's orbit, the scientists found Neptune in 1846. Following in the footsteps of these successful astronomers, Lowell calculated where in the sky he thought this new planet should be found based on Uranus's and Neptune's paths. Then he

In this photograph from 1912, Percival Lowell is shown in the observatory he built in Flagstaff, Arizona.

pointed his telescope in that direction. Lowell called the planet he was looking for "Planet X." But he never found it because he died suddenly in 1916 at the age of 61.

The search for Planet X did not end with Lowell's death, however. From 1925 to 1927, Percival Lowell's cousin and nephew struggled to raise enough money to have a special 13-inch (33-centimeter) telescope built and equipped with a camera. They planned to use the new, more powerful telescope to pursue Percival's dream of finding Planet X. Finally, A. Lawrence Lowell—Percival's brother and the president of Harvard University at the time—pledged the $10,000 needed to finish the telescope.

Tombaugh's Discovery

At about the same time, a young man from western Kansas named Clyde Tombaugh built a 9-inch (23-cm) telescope in his backyard from spare farm machinery and car parts. Tombaugh did not have any formal training in astronomy. He was a high-school graduate and an amateur astronomer. He spent his evenings gazing into the dark sky and making drawings of both Mars and Jupiter. In the fall of 1928, Tombaugh decided to send his sketches to the acting director of the Lowell Observatory, Dr. Vesto Slipher. Dr. Slipher was so impressed with what Tombaugh had been able to see with his handmade telescope that he offered Tombaugh a job. Tombaugh was specifically hired to operate the new telescope. He started in January 1929 and spent hours and hours photographing the night sky in the area where Lowell had calculated that Planet X should be.

By June of 1929, there were hundreds of images to compare. Using an instrument called a blink comparator that flips two photographs back and forth very rapidly, Tombaugh searched for moving points of light. When moving back and forth between images, distant stars stay in the same place. But because of the time difference between photographs and Earth's movement—which causes the viewing angle to change—objects that are closer to Earth seem to jump back and forth as they move in their orbits. If Tombaugh could find a point of light that had moved from one night to the next, it is possible that the object could be the missing Planet X he was looking for. During Tombaugh's time, "blinking" images required an enormous amount of patience and concentration.

Clyde Tombaugh is pictured with the telescope he built in 1928.

Today, computers have made the process a little easier.

In mid-February 1930, after ten long months and nearly 7,000 hours at the blink comparator, Clyde Tombaugh finally found two photographs, which were taken six days apart—on January 23 and January 29, 1930. He believed that they proved the existence of Lowell's Planet X. This made Tombaugh the first American to discover a planet. Although he found the planet in February, Tombaugh did not announce his findings to the scientific community until March 13, 1930. He waited because March 13 would have been Percival Lowell's seventy-fifth birthday.

After finding Pluto, Tombaugh did not stop looking for other planets. In 1932, he decided to enter Kansas University to work toward a college degree in astronomy. The university allowed Tombaugh to skip the beginning astronomy classes where other students learned about his discovery of Pluto. During the summers, he returned to the Lowell Observatory in Arizona and continued to compare many other photographs.

After earning his degree, Tombaugh returned to Flagstaff and the Lowell Observatory and continued his search until 1945. Between Pluto's discovery in 1930 and the time he left the Lowell Observatory fifteen years later, Tombaugh found hundreds of asteroids, two comets, one nova, and a lot of star clusters and

A portion of Tombaugh's observation notes shows where he noted that he discovered Lowell's Planet X.

other galaxies. However, he never did find any other planets. After leaving the Lowell Observatory, he went on to have a long and distinguished career in astronomy.

PLUTO'S NAME

Many names were suggested for Planet X. Percival Lowell's widow, Constance Lowell, suggested Zeus, Percival, Lowell, and Constance. The *New York Times* suggested the name Minerva. Another mythical name, Chronos, was also suggested. But the name that astronomers at the Lowell Observatory liked the best was suggested by an eleven-year-old girl named Venetia Burney.

Pluto, the Roman god of the underworld, is shown petting his three-headed dog, Cerberus. In Greek mythology, Pluto was known as Hades.

Venetia Burney was from Oxford, England, and she was very interested in mythology and astronomy. She suggested the name Pluto. Astronomers at the Lowell Observatory liked the fact that Pluto started with the letters "P" and "L," Percival Lowell's initials. The symbol astronomers use for Pluto combines the letters "P" and "L." According to Roman mythology, Pluto was the brother of the gods Jupiter, Neptune, and Juno. He was also the third son of Saturn and the Roman god of the underworld, or the dead. Pluto could also make himself invisible whenever he wanted to. Astronomers adopted the name Pluto for the ninth planet on March 24, 1930.

Pluto

This is the scientific symbol for the planet Pluto.

Scientists later found that the strange orbits of Uranus and Neptune, which prompted Lowell to look for the mysterious Planet X to begin with, did not really exist. Lowell's calculations were incorrect. It was just an amazing coincidence that his calculations pointed to the exact section of sky where Pluto lay. That coincidence combined with Tombaugh's amazing persistence at the blink comparator paid off with the discovery of a new planet.

2

PLUTO'S STRUCTURE AND FEATURES

Scientists think that most of Pluto is rock. However, about one-fourth of the planet is made of ice. The surface of Pluto is extremely cold. Scientists are not exactly sure how cold, but they think it must be somewhere between -378 and -396 degrees Fahrenheit (-228 and -238 degrees Celsius). The coldest temperature ever recorded on Earth was -128 degrees Fahrenheit (-89 degrees C) in Antarctica. So Pluto is much, much colder than even the coldest spot on Earth.

An illustration shows a view of Pluto (center) and Charon (right) from the surface of one of the dwarf planet's moons.

PLUTO'S ATMOSPHERE

Scientists believe that only some of the ice on Pluto is water ice—frozen water like ice on Earth. They have evidence that there are patches of other types of ice made of nitrogen, methane, and carbon monoxide on the surface of Pluto. Every two hundred years or so, when Pluto sneaks inside Neptune's orbit and gets closer to the Sun for about twenty years, some of these ice patches change from a solid into a gas. This creates a very thin atmosphere for Pluto. An atmosphere is a layer of gases that surround a planet.

Pluto's atmosphere is mostly nitrogen gas—just like Earth's atmosphere, which is 78 percent nitrogen. Titan, Saturn's largest moon, and Triton, Neptune's largest moon, also have mostly nitrogen atmospheres. Pluto, Earth, Titan, and Triton are the only four bodies in our Solar System that are known to have nitrogen-rich atmospheres. When Pluto goes back to its outside orbit, beyond Neptune, however, it gets very cold and its atmosphere falls back to the ground—similar to the way snow falls on Earth.

Scientists suspect that the snow and ice on Pluto's surface is relatively fresh. They think this because about 60 percent of the sunlight that reaches the surface of Pluto is reflected, or bounces back. This reflection makes Pluto brighter than other space bodies that do not reflect as much sunlight.

INSIDE PLUTO

Right now scientists believe that Pluto has a core made of solid rock. This rock core is probably surrounded by a thick layer of water ice. Their theory is that as Pluto formed, the rock, which is denser, or heavier for its size, sank to the center of the planet while less dense material, like the ice, rose to the top.

Scientists are not sure what Pluto is made of, but they believe that it has a rocky and icy core covered by a water ice layer, and surrounded by an atmosphere of gases, such as nitrogen and methane.

The water ice makes up Pluto's mantle. A planet's—or, in this case, a dwarf planet's—mantle is the layer between its core and its crust. The crust is the part you can see. Scientists believe that the inside of Pluto is warmer than its surface. That is because they think the interior of Pluto contains radioactive elements. These are elements that naturally break down, or decay. When radioactive elements decay, they give off radiation, or energy. This energy makes the inside of Pluto warmer than its surface. Between Pluto's rocky core and icy mantle, scientists wonder if there might not be a layer of melted ice. This would mean that just below the frozen surface of Pluto there may be a gigantic ocean! When the *Galileo* spaceship explored Jupiter and its moons, it sent back evidence that three of Jupiter's moons—Europa, Callisto, and possibly Ganymede—might also have underground oceans like the one thought to exist on Pluto.

Below the ocean, other scientists imagine that there may be a layer of organic—carbon-containing—chemicals. Organic chemicals are needed for life as we know it to exist. Water and a source of energy such as sunlight are needed, too. Other elements that are needed to build living things include phosphorus, sulfur, hydrogen, and oxygen. The hydrogen and oxygen are present in water. Even though the water on Pluto is frozen into ice, it still has hydrogen and oxygen in it and its chemical formula is the same as the formula for water on Earth. So it seems as if Pluto has at least some of the basic chemicals that make up living things—carbon, hydrogen, and oxygen. However, Pluto is extremely dark and cold, so it is unlikely that Pluto has or has had some form of life on it. But it is not impossible.

All of these are only theories for now. Scientists hope that the *New Horizons* spacecraft, which should arrive at Pluto in 2015, will give them a better idea about what makes up the inside of Pluto.

A SMALL, DARK ICE DWARF

At only 4,500 miles (7,242 km) around, Pluto is small, especially when compared to the circumference of Earth which is 24,901 miles (40,074 km) at the Equator. Pluto is so small that it could actually fit in the distance between Washington, D.C., and Denver, Colorado. Even our Moon is bigger than Pluto. Because the mass of a planet affects how much gravity it has, and Pluto is so much smaller than Earth, Pluto has just a fraction of Earth's gravity. This means that if you weigh 100 pounds (45 kilograms) on Earth, you would weigh not quite 7 pounds (3 kg) on Pluto.

Because Pluto is far from the Sun, it is very dark, too. Earth is 1 A.U., or about 93 million miles (149 million km), from the Sun.

An artist's depiction of Pluto's view of the Sun shows how dark the planet is because of its distance from the Sun.

Pluto, on the other hand, is about 39.5 A.U. away from the Sun. That is 3.67 billion miles (5.9 billion km). Because of the distance, the Sun would appear one thousand times dimmer on Pluto than it does on Earth. Even if the skies above Pluto are clear and cloud-free, it is much darker there than even a cloudy, stormy day on Earth.

Even though Pluto receives less sunlight than Earth, it does receive ultraviolet (UV) energy from the Sun. On Pluto, the UV rays cause chemical reactions in the atmosphere and create a thin layer of haze or smog around the planet. When the chemicals in this haze mix with the chemical snows that fall to the surface of Pluto, it gives the snow a light yellow or pink color that astronomers can see from Earth. Other areas of Pluto are dark grey. Scientists wonder if these areas might be rocky with no snow cover. They may also be areas made of material that has a lot of carbon in it. Either way, they think that these dark grey areas may have been formed when comets smashed into the surface of Pluto.

PLUTO'S ORBIT

Like Earth, Pluto has two poles—a North Pole and a South Pole. Pluto's axis, which is an imaginary line down through the center, goes through its North and South Poles, just as Earth's does. Pluto and Earth both rotate, or spin around, their axis. Earth spins on its axis once every twenty-four hours. This makes one Earth day. It takes almost six-and-a-half Earth days for Pluto to spin around its axis one time. That means that one Pluto day is around six Earth-days long.

As Earth moves around the Sun, its axis does not point straight up and down. Instead, Earth is tilted about 23.5 degrees. Pluto is also tilted on its axis. But Pluto is much more tilted than Earth. In fact, Pluto rotates around the Sun tilted at 120 degrees, which is practically on its side. This means that Pluto's North Pole does not point up but to the side. Only two planets in our Solar System do this—Pluto and Uranus.

It takes Earth a year—a little more than 365 days—to travel all the way around the Sun. Pluto, on the other hand, requires 248 Earth years to complete its trip. In other words, one Plutonian year takes 248 Earth years, or 90,520 days.

PLUTO'S MOONS

At one time, scientists believed that Pluto was much bigger than it actually is. This is because one of Pluto's moons, Charon, orbits Pluto very closely. In fact, Charon is only 10,000 to 12,000 miles (16,093 to 19,312 km) away from Pluto. Our Moon, on the other hand, is about 250,000 miles (402,336 km) from Earth. Because Charon was so close to Pluto, scientists at first did not realize that it was a separate body. They were including

COMPARING PLUTO AND EARTH

Earth (left), Pluto (center), and Charon (right)

	PLUTO	**EARTH**
DISTANCE FROM THE SUN	About 3.67 billion miles or (5.91 billion km)	93 million miles (149 million km)
SIZE	About 4,494 miles (7,232 km) around at its equator	7,926 miles (12,756 km) at the Equator
AVERAGE SURFACE TEMPERATURE	-378 to -396 degrees Fahrenheit (-228 to -237 degrees C)	60 degrees Fahrenheit (15 degrees C)
LENGTH OF YEAR	248 Earth years	365 days
LENGTH OF DAY	6.39 Earth days	24 hours
NUMBER OF MOONS	3	1
COMPOSITION OF PLANET	Carbon, hydrogen, oxygen	Mostly metals and rock
ATMOSPHERE	Mostly nitrogen, but also nitrogen, methane, and carbon monoxide	Mostly nitrogen and oxygen

the mass of Pluto's moon in with the mass of the planet. When Charon was discovered in 1978 and its mass subtracted, scientists discovered that Pluto was not only the smallest planet in our Solar System, but that it was smaller than seven moons in the Solar System, too. Saturn's moon Titan; Neptune's Triton; Jupiter's Ganymede, Callisto, Io, and Europa; and our own Moon all are bigger and more massive than Pluto.

In 1978, astronomers James Christy and Robert Harrington of the U.S. Naval Observatory were busy trying to figure out Pluto's exact path around the Sun when they discovered Charon. While studying photographs taken of Pluto, Christy noticed that the planet seemed to have a bump on its side. At first, Christy wondered if the telescope had been bumped while taking the pictures, smearing the image of Pluto. Christy also noticed that Pluto's "bump" seemed to travel around the planet. But every 6.39 days, it showed up in the same place. Christy also knew that 6.39 days is the exact period of time that it takes Pluto to make one complete turn around its axis—the length of a Plutonian day. To explain his observations, Christy came up with two hypotheses. Pluto either had a mountain on one side that was thousands of miles high or Pluto had a satellite orbiting it. After asking Harrington to check his observations, both of the scientists concluded that the blob in the photographs was indeed a satellite. Christy relied on Greek mythology to help him name the newly found satellite. In Greek mythology, Charon was a ferryman. He ferried the souls of the dead across the River of the Dead, which surrounds the underworld.

Charon, unlike most other satellites in our Solar System, is large in relation to the planet it orbits. Because of its size, Charon has enough gravity to affect the motion of Pluto. Most other satellites, like Earth's Moon, for example, are too small to affect the orbit of the planet that they revolve around. The ratio between the masses of Pluto and Charon is 8 to 1. That means that Pluto is only eight times more massive than Charon. For other planets and satellites, that mass ratio is more on the order of 10,000 to 1. In other words, some planets are 10,000 times more massive than their satellites.

The name *Charon* is fitting for a Plutonian moon, since Charon was the ferryman who transported souls to the underworld, the home of the god Pluto.

Scientists believe that Charon was formed when something hit Pluto and broke off chunks of the planet. These chunks eventually came together to make the moon. Scientists think that Charon is most likely structured in one of two ways. Its interior could be made up of a core of rock that is surrounded by a thick layer of ice, similar to the structure that they believe Pluto has. Or the ice and rock could be combined, forming a uniform rock-ice mixture all the way through. They also believe that Charon is covered in water ice that has ammonia mixed with it. Scientists think the ammonia-rich water ice is spewed onto the surface of the moon by volcanic-like eruptions from cracks in Charon's icy surface. Scientists call this process cryovolcanism. The prefix "cryo-" means cold. To really find out if their hypothesis is true, however, the scientists will have to wait for the *New Horizons* spacecraft to explore Pluto.

As Charon moves around Pluto, the satellite always presents the same face, or side, to Pluto. This is not that unusual. What is unusual about the way Charon and Pluto move around each other is that the same side of Pluto always faces Charon, too. Most other planets or bodies orbited by a satellite turn a different side to the moon as it moves around the planet. So if people could live on Pluto and they lived on the side of Pluto opposite Charon, they would never see the satellite. Likewise, a person living on the opposite side of Charon would never see Pluto. Even if the person lived on the side of Pluto where they could see Charon,

Compared to other planets and their moons, Charon is large in relation to the dwarf planet Pluto.

the moon would always appear to be in the same place. It would not rise, set, or move across the sky like our Moon does.

Because of their sizes and the way Charon and Pluto move around each other, scientists call the two of them a "double" or "binary planet." Pluto-Charon is the only binary dwarf planet in our Solar System so far. Scientists have found many binary stars, binary asteroids, and eight other binary objects in the Kuiper Belt. They suspect that there may be other binary planets in our galaxy, too.

Charon is not Pluto's only moon. The dwarf planet has two others—Hydra and Nix. Hydra and Nix were discovered in 2005 by the Hubble Space Telescope. Both satellites are much smaller than Charon. Because of the way Hydra and Nix orbit Pluto, scientists believe that they were formed by the same

A 2006 image from NASA shows the Hubble Space Telescope's view of Pluto and Charon (center) and the two smaller moons, Hydra and Nix.

huge collision that formed Charon rather than being objects captured by Pluto's gravitational force.

3

CHANGING PLUTO'S STATUS

Pluto is round like a planet and it orbits the Sun like a planet, so why is it not a planet anymore? As of August 24, 2006, the IAU defined a planet as a space body that has three qualities— it must orbit the Sun; it must have enough gravity to make it into a nearly round shape; and it must have cleared the area around its orbit of other smaller objects. Pluto meets the first two requirements, but it fails on the last one.

THE CONTROVERSY

The debate over Pluto's planetary status began in the scientific community in 2005, when a large **Kuiper Belt (KBO)** object called 2003 UB313 was found. With a diameter of about 1,500 miles

The decision to change Pluto's status from a regular planet to a dwarf planet is a controversial one. Not all scientists agree that it was the right thing to do.

(2,414 km), 2003 UB313 is larger than Pluto by about 60 miles (96 km). Then scientists found that 2003 UB313 is also 27 percent more massive than Pluto.

In 2006, scientists renamed 2003 UB313. Its new name is Eris, for the Greek goddess of warfare and conflict. Scientists gave the object this name because it caused so much disagreement in the scientific community. Some astronomers believed that if Pluto was a planet, then something larger and more massive than Pluto should be a planet, too. Other scientists argued that if Eris was called a planet, our Solar System would have ten planets instead of nine. Ten planets may not sound so bad, but scientists expect to find many other objects in the Kuiper Belt in the future. Some of these objects may be even bigger and more massive than either Pluto or Eris. What if scientists find ten more Kuiper Belt objects that are bigger than Pluto? Should they become planets, too? Should our Solar System have twenty planets? Should it have fifty? Some scientists say yes, others say no.

The dwarf planet Eris was originally called 2003 UB313, or Xena.

THE DECISION

The IAU decided that regular planets must meet those three characteristics related to gravity, orbit, and shape. Like Pluto, Eris passes the first two tests for planethood, but it fails the last one. Pluto and Eris both orbit the Sun in the debris-filled Kuiper Belt and are round. However, there are smaller bodies all around them, and Eris and Pluto cannot clear their orbit of the debris and smaller bodies. Therefore, the IAU named Pluto and Eris "dwarf planets." Some scientists also call the dwarf planets "minor planets."

Some scientists, such as Alan Stern, the chief National Aeronautics and Space Administration (NASA) scientist on the *New Horizons* mission to Pluto, do not like the new classification. Stern points out that, in the past, scientists have had no limits on the number of mountains or rivers that can be found and named. So why should planets be any different, Stern argues. But, for now, the IAU has decided that there are eight planets, and only eight planets, in our Solar System.

THE KUIPER BELT

As well as being called a dwarf planet or an ice dwarf, Pluto is also sometimes called a **trans-Neptunian object (TNO)**. TNOs are bodies that orbit the Sun beyond Neptune's orbit. There are

Pluto (and its moon Charon) are beyond Neptune's orbit, but are still affected by that planet's gravitational forces.

millions of TNOs. Scientists group TNOs by the way they orbit the Sun. If a TNO is under the influence of Neptune's gravity, it is classified as a Kuiper Belt object (KBO). Because Pluto is affected by Neptune's gravitational pull, it is designated as a KBO as well as a TNO.

The Kuiper Belt is a disc-shaped zone about 2.8 billion to 4.6 billion miles (4.5 to 7.4 billion km) from the Sun. Scientists call the 4.6-billion-mile (7.4-billion-km) mark the Kuiper cliff. Beyond that there is nearly empty space. Because most Kuiper Belt

A computer illustration shows that the Kuiper Belt is full of icy bodies and other small space bodies and debris.

objects are small—Eris is the biggest one, Pluto is the second largest—they appear as very dim stars even with the world's most powerful telescopes. Luckily for Clyde Tombaugh, Pluto is a bit of an exception because it reflects more sunlight than other KBOs. Most KBOs reflect about 4 to 20 percent, compared to Pluto's 60 percent. This makes Pluto, by far, the easiest KBO to see from Earth.

For a long time, scientists thought that Pluto and Charon were the only objects beyond Neptune. But in the 1950s, Gerard Kuiper, the astronomer who first suspected the existence of the zone that was later named for him, predicted that scientists would eventually find hundreds or thousands of objects just like Pluto. Indeed, in 1992, scientists found another object in the Kuiper Belt. They named it 1992 QB1. Since then, they have found at least one thousand more KBOs and they suspect that there are even more out there.

PLUTINOS, TWOTINOS, AND CUBEWANOS

All of the planets in our Solar System orbit the Sun in a counterclockwise direction on one plane. To help you picture it, imagine all of the planets traveling around the Sun in a circle, with the planets sitting on something like a flat tabletop. This

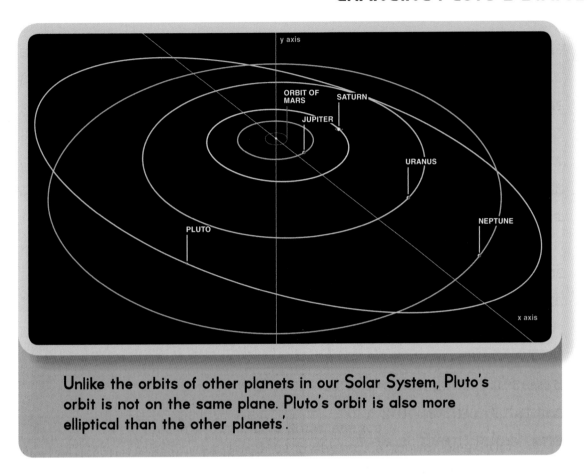

Unlike the orbits of other planets in our Solar System, Pluto's orbit is not on the same plane. Pluto's orbit is also more elliptical than the other planets'.

is a plane called the **plane of the ecliptic**. Pluto's orbit is less circular and more elliptical (oval-shaped) than most of the other planets' orbits. And Pluto's orbit is not along the same flat ecliptic plane that the planets follow. Pluto's orbit is tilted about 17 degrees out of the plane of the ecliptic. The strange tilt, and the fact that Pluto sometimes switches places with Neptune, makes Pluto's orbit quite bizarre when compared to the other planets or dwarf planets orbiting the Sun.

THE DWARF PLANET PLUTO

Pluto was the first KBO found with an elliptical orbit, and the first KBO that goes around the Sun twice for every three times Neptune does. This is called a 3:2 resonance with Neptune. Neptune's gravity influences Pluto to move around the Sun in this way. Since Pluto's discovery, other objects with elliptical orbits have been found in a 3:2 resonance with Neptune. In Pluto's honor, these objects are called **plutinos**. Huya, Ixion, Orcus, and Rhadamanthus are plutinos that scientists have found so far. A few KBOs go around the Sun only once for every two times Neptune does. In other words, they are in a 2:1 resonance with Neptune. These objects are sometimes called twotinos. Other KBOs that have nearly circular obits, are in the plane of the ecliptic, and do not have any kind of resonance with Neptune are called cubewanos. Chaos, Deucalion, Quaoar, and Varuna are examples of cubewanos.

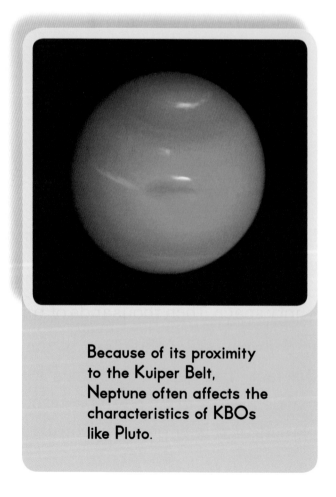

Because of its proximity to the Kuiper Belt, Neptune often affects the characteristics of KBOs like Pluto.

WHAT ELSE IS OUT THERE?

KBOs are not the only objects beyond Neptune. There are also scattered disk objects and the Oort Cloud. Scattered disk objects, like KBOs, are under the gravitational influence of Neptune. The difference between scattered disk objects and KBOs has to do with the way they orbit the Sun. KBOs have nonorderly orbits within, or close to, the plane of the ecliptic—the plane that the planets are on. Scattered disk objects, however, have nonorderly orbits that are tilted very differently from the plane of the ecliptic. These are much more tilted than Pluto's 17 degree out-of-plane orbit. This means that scattered disk objects can go way above and way below the plane of the ecliptic. Eris is a scattered disk object. It is tilted at a 44 degree angle to the plane of the ecliptic. Some scientists believe that scattered disk objects may have started out as KBOs, but were "scattered" further out of the Solar System, beyond the Kuiper Belt, when they got close to one of the gas giants.

Beyond the scattered disk objects is a wide area of almost empty space. Then thousands of times further from the Sun than Pluto and the other Kuiper Belt objects, is the Oort Cloud. The presence of the Oort Cloud was proposed by astronomer Jan Oort in 1950. Oort guessed that there was an area far from the Sun where the beginnings of long-period comets existed. Oort believed that every now and then one of these proto-comets—beginning

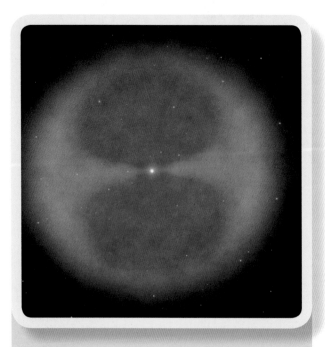

Scientists do not know what the Oort Cloud actually looks like, but many think that it could appear as a hazy cloud with the Sun in the center.

comets—was knocked into the inner solar system, possibly by some kind of collision. Scientists today agree. They believe that most of the long-period comets, the ones that come close enough to Earth to be seen only once every million years or so, probably come from the Oort Cloud.

Scientists hypothesize that the Oort Cloud is between 4 and 9 trillion miles (6.4 and 14.4 trillion km) from the Sun, or about a light-year away. But they have never actually seen the Oort Cloud because it is so far away. The most distant object seen by scientists so far is Sedna. But Sedna is only 88 billion miles (142 billion km) away from the Sun. Scientists sometimes call Sedna an "inner Oort Cloud" object. But they are not entirely certain what category Sedna really fits into yet. They do know that Sedna is so far from the Sun that it takes Sedna between 10,500 and 12,000 years to make one complete trip around the massive star.

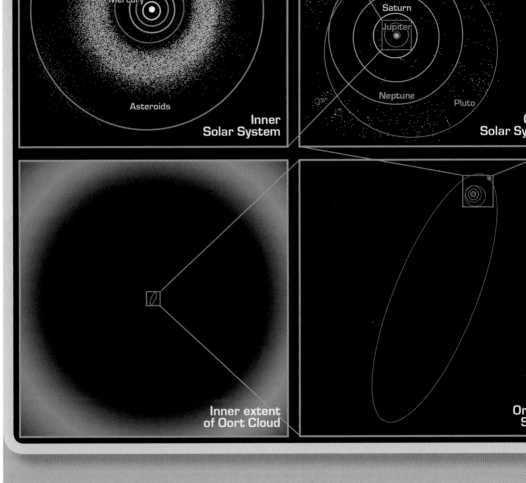

These four images show scientists' current understanding of
Sedna's location and orbit. The top images show Sedna's location
in relation to the planets in the Solar System. The bottom-right

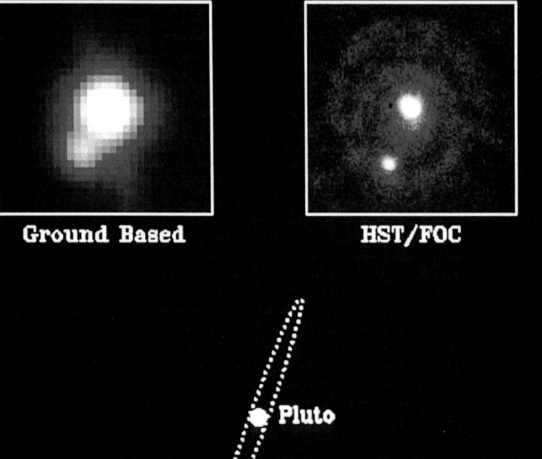

Ground Based

HST/FOC

Pluto

Charon

4

MISSION TO PLUTO

Because it is so far away, a spacecraft has not yet reached Pluto. But on January 19, 2006, NASA launched a robotic space probe called *New Horizons. New Horizons* is traveling to the Kuiper Belt.

Until *New Horizons* reaches Pluto, the only way scientists can see Pluto and other TNOs is by using Earth-based telescopes or Earth-orbiting satellite observatories like the Hubble Space Telescope. The best pictures scientists have of Pluto so far were taken by the Hubble, but they are very fuzzy. Scientists hope that *New Horizons* will be able to provide much better pictures of Pluto. *New Horizons* will not only photograph Pluto and Charon, it will also map the surface of the dwarf planet and its moon.

So far, the clearest images ever taken of Pluto and its moons were from the Hubble Space Telescope. The image in the upper left shows what Pluto and Charon look like from a strong ground-based telescope. The image in the upper right displays Pluto and Charon as it is viewed by the Hubble's FOC, or Faint Object Camera.

THE DWARF PLANET PLUTO

Built by Johns Hopkins University's Applied Physics Laboratory, in Laurel, Maryland, *New Horizons* is the fastest spacecraft ever built. By February 2007, a little more than a year after it was launched, *New Horizons* passed Jupiter. At its closest point, Jupiter is about 391 million miles (629 million km) from Earth. By contrast, the *Galileo* spacecraft, which was launched on October, 18, 1989, required six years to reach Jupiter.

When *New Horizons'* engines were turned off, the spacecraft was traveling at 36,000 miles (57,936 km) per hour. As it approached Jupiter, the space probe used Jupiter's gravity to help it pick up even more speed. This maneuver is called a gravity assist. The boost in speed given to *New Horizons* by Jupiter's gravitational field will save the spacecraft three years on its journey to Pluto. In the process, the spacecraft also gave NASA scientists new information about Jupiter.

The *New Horizons* spacecraft flew past Jupiter (upper right) in 2007. Using the giant planet's gravity like a slingshot, the spacecraft will move farther into outer space to fly by Pluto and enter the Kuiper Belt. The Sun, Mercury, Venus, and Earth are shown to the left of the spacecraft.

STUDYING PLUTO'S ATMOSPHERE

Scientists expect *New Horizons* to reach Pluto in 2015. When it gets there, scientists hope to use instruments on the spacecraft to find out exactly what Pluto's atmosphere is made of, what its temperature is, and how much pressure it exerts on the dwarf planet. In the last decade, Pluto has started moving away from the Sun. In these last ten years, its atmosphere has gotten thicker. Eventually, as Pluto moves further from the Sun's warmth, the dwarf planet will get colder. When it gets cold enough, scientists expect the gases in Pluto's atmosphere to condense—change from gas into liquid—and freeze back into the frozen frosts that coat the surface of Pluto. The scientists do not know exactly when in Pluto's orbit this will happen, so they are eager to get *New Horizons* to Pluto as fast as possible. They hope it gets there before the atmosphere completely disappears again.

Scientists believe that Pluto's atmosphere is being lost to space. In fact, they think 100 to 1,000 pounds (45.3 to 453 kg) of Plutonian atmospheric gas is being sucked away from the dwarf planet every second. Pluto is losing its atmosphere because it does not have enough gravity to hold the gases in place. This happens to comets, too. However, Pluto is about 100 times bigger than most comets. And the gases that trail comets are blown

A scientist uses a model of the SWAP to explain how *New Horizons* will analyze Pluto's atmosphere.

away 100 to 1,000 times faster than Pluto's atmospheric gases are escaping.

Scientists hope that *New Horizons* will help them determine exactly how the solar winds affect Pluto and its atmosphere. They are specifically interested in how quickly the gas particles are leaving Pluto's atmosphere. If the gases are escaping the grip of the icy dwarf faster than 100 pounds per second, Pluto will have more in common with comets. However, if the gases are leaving at a slower pace, Pluto would more closely resemble the planets Mars and Venus. Either way, an instrument aboard *New Horizons* called SWAP, which stands for the Solar Wind Around Pluto, is set to measure how the solar winds are traveling past Pluto.

Another instrument called the Pluto Energetic Particle Spectrometer Science Investigation, or PEPSSI, will measure the exact gases that are escaping from the atmosphere of Pluto. Scientists believe that Earth's original atmosphere, which was made up of the elements hydrogen and helium, escaped the grip of Earth's gravity a long time ago, too. They hope to be able to figure out how this happened to Earth's early atmosphere by studying what is happening to Pluto's atmosphere.

Scientists also hope that *New Horizons* will be able to study the cores of Pluto and its moons. Scientists think that the new, clearer pictures *New Horizons* takes when it arrives will help them measure the mass, density, and shape of Pluto and Charon more exactly. This new information will provide them with better clues about the interior structure of both objects.

PLUTO AND TRITON—TWINS?

Until *New Horizons* arrives at Pluto, scientists can only make educated guesses about what the surface of Pluto really looks like. To help form the image they have of Pluto now, scientists looked at other bodies in the Solar System that they think have similar features to Pluto. Earth, for example, would not make a good model for what Pluto may look like because it is much closer to the Sun. Neptune, the planet that is closest to Pluto will not work as a model either because it is a giant gas planet. But Neptune's largest moon, Triton, seems to be a good model for Pluto.

Like Pluto, scientists believe that Triton has a rocky core with an icy covering. Scientists know from pictures sent back by the *Voyager* spacecraft that Triton has a dark region around its

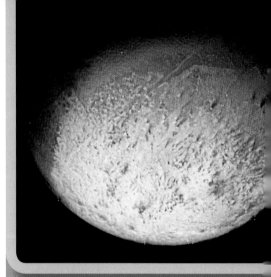

equator (middle) and brighter areas at its poles, just like the pictures they have of Pluto. Triton also has the same nitrogen-rich atmosphere Pluto does.

Because of the way Triton orbits Neptune, some scientists do not believe that Neptune's moon was formed by a collision, like Pluto's satellite, Charon, was. Instead, they believe that Triton may have started out as a Kuiper Belt object that traveled too close to Neptune and was captured by the giant planet's gravity. Because

Triton, Neptune's largest moon, is shown here from a 1989 photograph from the spacecraft *Voyager 2*. Scientists think that Triton and Pluto may share many of the same characteristics.

of the similarities between Triton and Pluto, scientists think they may look a lot alike.

NAMES FLYING TO PLUTO

Before launching the *New Horizons* spacecraft, NASA asked people to send in their names. They put all 430,000 names that were submitted on a compact disc that is now winging its way toward Pluto on *New Horizons*.

THE FUTURE

In June and early July of 1994, the Hubble Space Telescope mapped about 85 percent of the surface of Pluto. From the Hubble images beamed back, scientists were able to identify twelve different dark and light regions on the surface of the icy dwarf. However, the images that scientists are working with are very fuzzy, which makes it hard to see the differences in the surface texture. However, they have been able to distinguish a dark band around the equator of Pluto and bright polar caps.

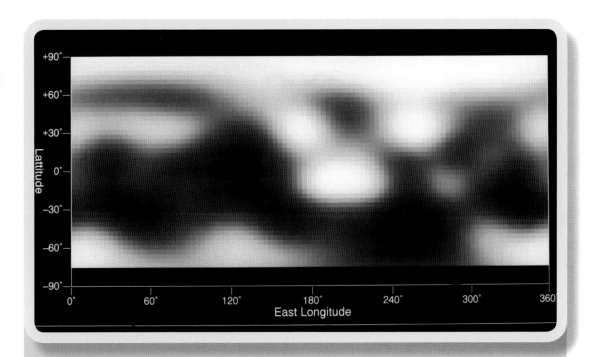

The Hubble Space Telescope's Faint Object Camera gave scientists a better look at Pluto's surface. Clearer images may be available once *New Horizons* reaches the dwarf planet.

THE DWARF PLANET PLUTO

Scientists think that these areas may be the result of different geological features such as mountains, valleys, and basins. These features may also be recent impact craters from space objects that crash into Pluto. Another possibility that could explain the different surface textures is different thickness and types of frosts. These frosts, made mostly of nitrogen with some methane, appear and disappear as the seasons change on Pluto. The astronomers working on the *New Horizons* mission are looking forward to getting clearer, more detailed pictures and data from the spacecraft. They may name some of the larger regions of Pluto's surface in the future.

After leaving Pluto, *New Horizons* will go on to explore other objects in the Kuiper Belt. Scientists have already discovered more than 1,000 Kuiper Belt objects beyond the orbit of Jupiter. They

When *New Horizons* goes beyond Pluto and enters the Kuiper Belt, scientists can only guess at what kinds of wonders it will discover.

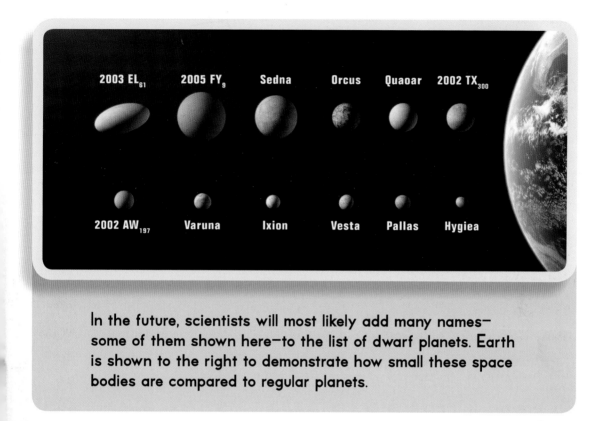

2003 EL₆₁ 2005 FY₉ Sedna Orcus Quaoar 2002 TX₃₀₀

2002 AW₁₉₇ Varuna Ixion Vesta Pallas Hygiea

In the future, scientists will most likely add many names—some of them shown here—to the list of dwarf planets. Earth is shown to the right to demonstrate how small these space bodies are compared to regular planets.

think that there are still more than 500,000 additional KBOs out there that are 20 miles (32 km) across or more. There are probably many, many smaller objects out there as well, just waiting to be discovered.

Further into the future, astronomers would also like to learn more about Sedna, the so-called inner Oort Cloud object that is 90 billion miles (145 billion km) away from the Sun. Even though *New Horizons* is the fastest spaceship ever launched, explorations of Sedna will require something even faster. But we will get there—one day.

QUICK FACTS ABOUT PLUTO

NAME AND ORIGIN OF NAME: Pluto, the Roman god of the underworld

YEAR OF DISCOVERY AND DISCOVERER: Discovered in 1930 by Clyde Tombaugh

PLANETARY STATUS: Dwarf planet

SIZE: About 4,494 miles (7,232 km) around at the equator

DISTANCE FROM EARTH: About 2.66 billion miles (4.28 billion km) or 38.482 A.U.

DISTANCE FROM THE SUN: About 3.67 billion miles (5.9 billion km) or 39.482 A.U.

NUMBER OF MOONS: Three—Charon, Hydra, and Nix

LENGTH OF DAY: 6.39 Earth days

LENGTH OF YEAR: About 248 Earth years

AVERAGE SURFACE TEMPERATURE: About −378 to −396 degrees Fahrenheit (−228 to −238 degrees C)

GLOSSARY

asteroid —Rocky bodies that mainly orbit the Sun between Mars and Jupiter.

astronomer —A scientist who studies stars, planets, and other objects in space.

atmosphere—A layer of gases that surrounds a planet.

comet—An object made up of ice, frozen gases, and dust. Comets pass close to the Earth at regular intervals.

galaxy —A group of stars, dust, and gas held together by gravity. Our Solar System is in the Milky Way galaxy.

gravity—A force that attracts one object to another. Objects with more mass have stronger gravitational pull on other objects. Distance between objects can also affect gravity.

Kuiper Belt—A disc-shaped zone about 2.8 billion to 4.6 billion miles (4.5 billion km to 7.4 billion km) from the Sun.

Kuiper Belt object (KBO)—A space body that orbits the Sun beyond Neptune's orbit, but is under the influence of Neptune's gravity.

light-year —The number of miles that light can travel in one year—about 6 trillion miles (9.7 trillion km).

mass—The amount of matter in an object.

matter —Anything that has mass and takes up space.

meteoroid—Rocky bodies smaller than asteroids orbiting the Sun.

orbit—To travel around something in a set and somewhat circular path. An orbit is the path a planet, moon, or other celestial body takes around another object.

plane of the ecliptic—The flat, tabletop-like path the planets follow around the Sun.

plutinos —Objects with an elliptical orbit that are in a 3:2 resonance with Neptune.

trans-Neptunian object (TNO)—A space body that orbits the Sun beyond Neptune's orbit.

weight—A measurement of the gravitational pull on an object.

FIND OUT MORE

BOOKS

Aguilar, David. *11 Planets: A New View of the Solar System*. Washington, D.C.: National Geographic Society, 2008.

---. *Planets, Stars, and Galaxies: A Visual Encyclopedia of Our Universe*. Washington, D.C.: National Geographic Society, 2008.

Barnes-Svarney, Patricia. *A Traveler's Guide to the Solar System*. New York, NY: Sterling Publishing, 2008.

Graham, Ian. *Stars and Galaxies*. Mankato, MN: Black Rabbit Books, 2007.

Landau, Elaine. *Beyond Pluto: The Final Frontier in Space*. New York, NY: Children's Press, 2008.

---. *Pluto: From Planet to Dwarf*. New York, NY: Children's Press, 2008.

Loewen, Nancy. *Dwarf Planets: Pluto, Charon, Ceres and Eris*. Minneapolis, MN: Coughlan Publishing, 2008.

McCutcheon, Marc. *The Kid Who Named Pluto: And the Stories of Other Extraordinary Young People in Science*. San Francisco, CA: Chronicle Books, 2008.

Scott, Elaine. *When Is a Planet Not a Planet?: The Story of Pluto*. Boston, MA: Houghton Mifflin Company, 2007.

WEBSITES

CoolCosmos: Pluto
http://coolcosmos.ipac.caltech.edu/cosmic_kids/AskKids/pluto.shtml

Curious about Astronomy? Ask an Astronomer
http://curious.astro.cornell.edu

NASA Kids' Club
http://www.nasa.gov/audience/forkids/kidsclub/flash/index.html

NASA Solar System Exploration for Kids
http://solarsystem.nasa.gov/kids/index.cfm

NASA Space Place: Pluto
http://spaceplace.nasa.gov/en/kids/pluto/index.shtml

National Geographic Kids: Is Pluto No Longer a Planet?
http://kids.nationalgeographic.com/Stories/SpaceScience/Pluto-planet

NEW HORIZONS
http://pluto.jhuapl.edu

The ~~Nine~~ 8 Planets—Just for Kids
http://kids.nineplanets.org/

Pluto: A Dwarf Planet
http://starchild.gsfc.nasa.gov/docs/StarChild/solar_system_level2/pluto.html

Pluto: Frequently Asked Questions
http://pluto.jhuapl.edu/overview/faqs.php

Pluto and Charon: A Family Album
http://pluto.jhuapl.edu/science/everything_pluto/5_looks.php?selectedImage=image08.php

BIBLIOGRAPHY

The author found these resources especially helpful while researching this book.

Alexander, Amir. "Measurement of Eris's Mass Reignites Planetary Debate." http://www.planetary.org/news/2007/0619_Measurement_of_Eriss_Mass_ Reignites.html

Buie, Marc. "Surface Temperature of Pluto." http://www.lowell.edu/users/buie/ pluto/plutotemp.html#TOP

Corfield, Richard. *Lives of the Planets*. New York, NY: Basic Books, 2007.

Darling, David. "Eris (Minor Planet 136199)." http://www.daviddarling.info/ encyclopedia/E/Eris.html

Harvey, Samantha. "Solar System Exploration: Pluto" http://solarsystem.nasa.gov/ planets/profile.cfm?Object=Pluto&Display=Overview

International Astronomical Union, The. "About IAU." http://www.iau.org/about

Johns Hopkins University Applied Physics Laboratory. "Colossal Cousin to a Comet?" Rhttp://pluto.jhuapl.edu/science/everything_pluto/8_cousin.php

Lakdawalla, Emily. "Ice Crystals on Pluto's Moon Charon Suggests a Surface Constantly Refreshed by Ammonia-Water Volcanoes." http://www.planetary. org/news/2007/0718_Ice_Crystals_on_Plutos_Moon_Charon.html

NASA. "NASA Spacecraft Sees Changes in Jupiter System." http://solarsystem. nasa.gov/news/display.cfm?News_ID=23556

Planetary Society, The. "Trans-Neptunian Objects." http://www.planetary.org/ explore/topics/trans_neptunian_objects

Rieke, George, and Marcia Rieke. "Beyond the Planets—the Discovery of Pluto." http://ircamera.as.arizona.edu/NatSci102/lectures/pluto.htm

Sobel, Dava. *The Planets*. New York, NY: Viking, 2005.

Tombaugh, Clyde. "The Struggles to Find the Ninth Planet." http://pagesperso- orange.fr/olivier.granier/meca/vulga/pluton/pluton.htm

Weintraub, David. *Is Pluto a Planet?: A Historical Journey Through the Solar System*. Princeton, NJ: Princeton University Press, 2007.

INDEX

Page numbers in **boldface** indicate photos or illustrations.

ABOUT THE AUTHOR

Kristi Lew is the author of more than twenty science books for teachers and young people. Fascinated with science from a young age, she studied biochemistry and genetics in college. Before she started writing full time, she worked in genetic laboratories for more than ten years and taught high-school science. When she is not writing, she enjoys sailing with her husband, Simon, aboard their small sailboat, *Proton*. She lives, writes, and sails in St. Petersburg, Florida.